TE

**By the same author**

*Collected Poems 1987*

*Selected Poems 1990*

*Under the Circumstances* (1991)

*Old Men and Comets* (1993)

*Interplay: A Kind of Commonplace Book*
(1995, Oxford Paperbacks 1997)

**Editor of**

*The Oxford Book of Death*

*The Oxford Book of Friendship*
(with David Rawlinson)

*The Oxford Book of the Supernatural*

D. J. ENRIGHT

*Telling Tales*

PARADISE ILLUSTRATED
&
A FAUST BOOK

Oxford   New York
OXFORD UNIVERSITY PRESS
1997

*Oxford University Press, Great Clarendon Street, Oxford* OX2 6DP
*Oxford New York
Athens Auckland Bangkok Bogota Bombay Buenos Aires
Calcutta Cape Town Dar es Salaam Delhi Florence Hong Kong
Istanbul Karachi Kuala Lumpur Madras Madrid Melbourne
Mexico City Nairobi Paris Singapore Taipei Tokyo Toronto
and associated companies in
Berlin Ibadan*

*Oxford is a trade mark of Oxford University Press*

Telling Tales *with Foreword* © D. J. Enright *1997*

Paradise Illustrated *first published by
Chatto & Windus (1978), then in*
Collected Poems *by Oxford University Press (1981, 1987)*
A Faust Book *first published by Oxford University Press (1979),
then in* Collected Poems *(1981, 1987)*

*This edition of* Paradise Illustrated *with* A Faust Book
*published in Oxford Poets as* Telling Tales
*as an Oxford University Press paperback 1997*

*All rights reserved. No part of this publication may be reproduced,
stored in a retrieval system, or transmitted, in any form or by any means,
without the prior permission in writing of Oxford University Press.
Within the UK, exceptions are allowed in respect of any fair dealing for the
purpose of research or private study, or criticism or review, as permitted
under the Copyright, Designs and Patents Act, 1988, or in the case of
reprographic reproduction in accordance with the terms of the licences
issued by the Copyright Licensing Agency. Enquiries concerning
reproduction outside these terms and in other countries should be
sent to the Rights Department, Oxford University Press,
at the address above*

*This book is sold subject to the condition that it shall not, by way
of trade or otherwise, be lent, re-sold, hired out or otherwise circulated
without the publisher's prior consent in any form of binding or cover
other than that in which it is published and without a similar condition
including this condition being imposed on the subsequent purchaser*

*British Library Cataloguing in Publication Data
Data available*

*Library of Congress Cataloging in Publication Data
Data available*

*ISBN 0-19-288029-2*

1 3 5 7 9 10 8 6 4 2

*Printed in Hong Kong*

# Contents

*Foreword*     vii

PARADISE ILLUSTRATED     1

A FAUST BOOK     25

# Foreword

## *Paradise Illustrated* (1978)

A writer cannot tell readers what he has done, but only what he meant to do or what he thinks he has done. And he can always tell, for what it's worth, how he came about it, or how it came about.

On this last point: around 1974, while I was compiling a choice of Milton's verse, it struck me with greater force than ever before that in *Paradise Lost*, despite its grand style and momentous intention (to 'assert Eternal Providence, and justify the ways of God to men'), Milton had managed quite adroitly, if not to explain *why* we humans are as we are, at least to describe *how* we are. Perverse and our own worst enemies, it may be, or in Faustian fashion, never satisfied with what we have and blind to the possibility that the better is the enemy of the good. Samuel Johnson allowed that, by virtue of its subject, *Paradise Lost* had the advantage of being universally and perpetually interesting. 'All mankind will, through all ages, bear the same relation to Adam and to Eve, and must partake of that good and evil which extend to themselves.'

Out of that lengthy reading came a short sequence of poems touching, in a fairly homely way, on the course of events from Adam's first duty, the naming of the animals, the creation of the first woman (ostensibly the cause of all our woe, though some would say it was written in the stars), and man's first disobedience, to the expulsion from Eden and subsequent developments and foreshadowings. Primal innocence is a condition that even Milton could not convey at much length or in much detail; it was something barely describable in our language, something which was bound to end (or so we think in the wisdom of hindsight), and from such heights there could only be a great fall. For the story to engage and hold our interest, its human characters had to be human and fallible, like us. Yet what was lost, however impossible to conceive, stays with us as an elusive, cloudy memory, perhaps surfacing briefly at unpredictable moments and in scraps of dreams, persisting as an ideal with the value ascribed to ideals.

Seemingly there was no humour, no comedy in Paradise, certainly no irony. These are 'fallen' qualities or devices which humankind was to need desperately in post-Edenic life. I have attempted to introduce them both earlier and later, through Eve's unfortunate, though innocent, choice of 'Adam's apple' as a flower name, and Adam's linguistic anachronisms, as when alluding, after the extraction of his rib, to the anaesthetic. And similarly his disconcerting proposals, whether ominous or trivial or inadvertently indecent, of 'Indo-China', 'Bambi', 'Krafft-Ebing' (*Psychopathia Sexualis*, 1886), and 'Bollock' as apt epithets for the animals, and his play on words like 'baby' and 'brood': 'I think of words, therefore I am.' God is taken aback: his creature already shows signs of breaking away, of (an ambiguous expression) growing up. That, being omniscient, he knew this would happen poses a theological crux and adds to the irony. Was original sin even more original, or aboriginal, than has been assumed?

In *Areopagitica*, his defence of the freedom of the press, Milton asserted that he could not 'praise a cloistered virtue, unexercised and unbreathed, that never sallies out and sees her adversary'. For all his plain interdictions and warnings, it might appear that neither could God. In *Paradise Lost* Eve is endowed with sparks of distinctly postlapsarian wit; when Adam reproves her for wandering off alone and falling into the Serpent's ambush, she snaps back: 'Was I to have never parted from thy side?/As good have grown there still a lifeless rib.' (Yes, we tell ourselves, this is where we came in.) In an essay on theodicy Margarita Stocker has remarked that at a similar juncture my Eve is 'characterized in cognizance of contemporary feminism'. (If so, it hasn't prevented the odd reader from taking umbrage at the 'patriarchal' casting of blame, yet again, on the woman.) It wasn't feminism that I had in mind, but merely elementary justice; far from proposing a division (as against a distinction) between the sexes, let alone pitting one against the other, I wanted to keep them together, where they belong. If anything, God (I suspect) favoured Eve, for Adam, as Milton the expert portrays him, was too much the eager, compliant adjutant.

At all events, it was Eve who saw to it that a world lay all before them and they must choose their way, making use of whatever knowledge would now be theirs. Adam followed for a good — one is tempted to say divine — reason: he loved her. Thus, in a sense, obeying the Lord's injunction early in Genesis, that a man should leave his father and mother and cleave to his wife. 'Whether boon or curse'/'For better or for worse', is how this particular couple put it, as if intent on justifying the ways of men and women to God.

## *A Faust Book* (1979)

For their authors, at any rate, verse sequences hold out a particular charm. They combine the pleasure of writing poetry with the pleasure of telling a story, while freeing the writer from the necessity, imposed on the novelist, of unbroken narrative and sometimes tedious explanations. For this reason, *A Faust Book* soon followed *Paradise Illustrated*, though it was also the outcome of a lifelong interest in the Faust legend in its many avatars, from the Frankfurt *Historia von D. Johann Fausten* of 1587 and Marlowe's play, through puppet plays and parodies and Goethe's drama, to Thomas Mann's novel, *Doctor Faustus* (1947), in which Leverkühn is both a possessed, Nietzschean composer and emblematic of the rise and fall of the Third Reich.

Faust's sin corresponds to that of Adam and Eve. According to the Book of Genesis, in the Garden of Eden the Serpent told Eve that if they ate of the fruit of the forbidden tree, 'then your eyes shall be opened, and ye shall be as gods, knowing good and evil'. (The issue is explicitly and tendentiously noted by Mephistopheles here: 'They lost a garden, but they found a world.') This sin — if sin it is — was committed by Faust more deliberately, as would be expected of a discontented and ambitious scholar of his time, thirsting for deeper knowledge, whether forbidden or not, and the power it would bring him. To pledge his soul to the devil in exchange seemed a good bargain: a man whom Goethe represents as emending the opening words of the Gospel of St John, 'In the beginning was the Word', to 'In the beginning was the Deed', isn't going to be intimidated by what he sees, somewhat inconsistently, as a vulgar and outmoded bugbear from the Dark Ages.

While the Faust repertory embraces pity and terror, as well as righteous denunciation, it has commonly abounded in popular entertainment — crude horseplay, pranks, and ludicrous fiascos. Scholars find it difficult to believe that the buffoonery in Marlowe's play could come from his hand, though it can be argued that these low passages, adapted from the first Faust-book (as was the false wine conjured up in Goethe's tavern scene), serve as a mocking and orthodoxly Christian gloss on Faustus's claim that 'A sound magician is a mighty god.' One old theory identifies Faust with Johann Fust, a figure associated with the invention of printing, plainly one of the black arts. Daniel Defoe has it that Fust printed copies of the Psalter, marketed them as original manuscripts, and came close to being hanged for it. In my version the black art is held responsible for calamitous historical misprints in various editions of the Bible.

Inevitably Mephistopheles gets most of the best lines, not least in his cajoling remark to Faust: 'God moves in a mysterious manner — unlike me. Me you can understand.' It is foremost in his brief — he represents the Great Adversary — to discredit man's finer feelings and reduce his noble aspirations to dust and ashes. 'I am the spirit that always denies,' says Goethe's Mephistopheles in a forthright moment. And Faust's protestations of love for Gretchen end in the killing of her mother and brother, the drowning of her baby, and her own miserable death. While continuing to exploit possibilities for comedy and even slapstick, a modern treatment is more likely to dwell on science and technology — which once would have been deemed 'forbidden knowledge' — and their equivocal consequences, the 'necromantic' entertainment offered by television and video, and the sort of bleak prophecies uttered by Mephistopheles (cf. the proleptic disasters exuberantly listed by Adam, directly after sharing the fatal fruit: 'Donner-und-Blitzen, coups-de-foudre, infernos . . .').

Presumptuous blasphemer or Promethean hero? Marlowe had already moved some way from the original conception of the story as a pious and dreadful warning, by securing a strong measure of our sympathy for Faustus, notably through the great final lament. His play is entitled a 'Tragical History', in contrast to its probable source, the 'Damnable Life' of the English version of the *Historia*.

Even so, the man had to be duly punished and dragged down into hell: wherever Marlowe's personal sympathies lay, this made a tremendous finale. Goethe, an indefatigable seeker after knowledge and a believer in its holiness, couldn't possibly follow suit, and at the end of his huge and heterogeneous work he went to some pains, not to say dodgy devices, to redeem his hero, ending with a mystical extravaganza which my Mephistopheles derides for its lack of realism and relevance.

Loose and capacious as the legend is, amenable to diverse uses, it must in any treatment have some sort of conclusion. Bowing to the *Zeitgeist*, if a mite reluctantly, and similarly deterred from consigning Faust to damnation, I arranged for him to be rescued by a certain sophistical privy councillor from Weimar, on the Goethean grounds that though he had indeed gone astray, he had at least striven: and the Lord God himself had declared that 'While man still strives, still must he stray.' The best I could do was to allow Lucifer to save face by invoking the sprat and mackerel theory: 'We let the Doctor go scot-free, to encourage the others.' A flimsy pretext and an unconvincing ploy? But it doesn't do to make light of the devil.

D.J.E., 1997

# PARADISE ILLUSTRATED

# PARADISE ILLUSTRATED

I

'Come!' spoke the Almighty to Adam.
'There's work to do, even in Eden.'

'I want to see what you'll call them,'
The Lord said. 'It's a good day for it.'
'And take your thumb out of your mouth,'
He added. (Adam was missing his mother.)

So they shuffled past, or they hopped,
Or they waddled. The beasts of the field
And the fowls of the air,
Pretending not to notice him.

'Speak up now,' said the Lord God briskly.
'Give each and every one the name thereof.'

'Fido,' said Adam, thinking hard,
As the animals went past him one by one,
'Bambi', 'Harpy', 'Pooh',
'Incitatus', 'Acidosis', 'Apparat',
'Krafft-Ebing', 'Indo-China', 'Schnorkel',
'Buggins', 'Bollock' –

'Bullock will do,' said the Lord God, 'I like it.
The rest are rubbish. You must try again tomorrow.'

## II

'What a dream!' said Adam waking.
'I never dreamt a dream like that before.'

'You will,' remarked the Voice Divine, 'You will.'
'And worse,' He added *sotto Voce*,
Finding it hard to speak in accents mild,
Knowing what He knew.

('Why can't I ever live in the present?'
He would grumble. 'Never in the present.')

'You're luckier than I,' the Almighty said.
'I know of no one fit to shake My hand,
Let alone My equal. I'm on My own.'

'You're different,' said Adam,
'You don't need it.'
'It's wearing off,' said Adam,
'The anaesthetic.'

'Anaesthetic? What's a man like you
To do with words like that?'
He found it hard to speak in accents mild,
Knowing what He knew.

'You promised, Lord,'
Urged Adam. 'You promised me.'

'Behold her, not far off,
Flesh of your flesh, bone of your bone,'
Said He in neutral tones,
'Your madam, Adam,'
Knowing what He knew.


## III

'Rich soil,' remarked the Landlord.
'Lavishly watered.' Streams to the right,
Fountains to the left.
'The rose, you observe, is without a thorn.'

'What's a thorn?' asked Adam.
'Something you have in your side,'
The Landlord replied.

'And since there are no seasons
All the flowers bloom all the time.'

'What's a season?' Eve inquired.
'Yours not to reason why,'
The Landlord made reply.

Odours rose from the trees,
Grapes fell from the vines,
The sand was made of gold,
The pebbles were made of pearls.

'I've never seen the like,' said Eve.
'Naturally,' the Landlord smiled.

'It's unimaginable!' sighed Adam.
'You're not obliged to imagine it,'
Snapped the Landlord. 'Yet.'


IV

If you wanted ice-cream
There was ice-cream galore
Oozing from handy ice-plants.

(But you didn't really want ice-cream:
The weather wasn't hot enough.)

If you wanted a piping hot bath
There was piping hot water
Running in convenient brooks.

(But you didn't really want a piping hot bath:
The weather wasn't cold enough.)

If you wanted petrol
There was petrol in plenty
A few inches under the Garden.

(But what was the need for petrol?
There was nowhere you wanted to go.)

If you wanted money
Money grew on trees
(But what would you do with money?).

'But Adam wants me,' Eve told herself.
Adam told himself, 'But Eve needs me.'


V

    *'About them frisking played*
    *All beasts of th'earth . . .'*

'If we have a baby,
That elephant will have to go –
He's too unwieldy.'

'What's a baby?'
'A word I've just made up,'
Said Adam smugly.

'If we have a child,
That bear will have to go –
He's wild.'

'What's a child?'
'A word I've just made up,'
He smiled.

'If we have a brood,
That ape will have to go –
He's very rude.'

'What's a brood?'
'A word I've just made up,'
He cooed.

She said:
'But won't the wolf lie down with the lamb?'
He said:
'I think of words, therefore I am.'

## VI

'Can't you let *her* name something?'
Begged Adam. 'She's always on at me
About the animals.'

'Herself a fairer flower,'
Murmured God. 'Hardly necessary,
I would say. But if it makes her happy . . .'

*

'What a trek!' Eve muttered.
'The animals *came* to Adam . . .
Well, Mohammed must go to the mountain.'

'What's that you said?' the Almighty asked.
But she was on her way.

*

'Lady's finger,' said Eve.
'Lady's smock.
Lady's slipper.
Lady's tresses . . .'

She paused.
'Adam's apple.'

'No,' said the Lord,
'Strike that out.'

'Old man's beard, then.'
She sped towards the mountain.

'Lily.
Rose.
Violet.
Daisy.
Poppy.
Amaryllis.
Eglantine.
Veronica.
Marigold.
Iris.
Marguerite.
Pansy.
Petunia.

Jasmine.
May.'

'I'm worn out,' she gasped.
'Belladonna –
And that's all for today.'

*

'She's better at names than you were,'
The Lord observed.
'They all sound womanish to me,'
Said Adam, nettled.


## VII

To whom, indignantly, the Angel thus:
'Whereas by definition we are happy,
And happiness can only dwell with love –
My drift you follow, I presume?
In fact it's better than it is with you,
Since not a joint or membrane comes between.
Total we mix, we mix without restraint,
Easier than air with air, you have my word!'
    To whom thus Adam made reply:
'Too airy-fairy for the likes of me.
Myself I like a touch of flesh and blood,
Firm mounds to get my hands around.
Sex in the bed for me, not in the head.'
    To which said Raphael with contracted brow:
'If touch be what you're wild about,
Consider this: the cattle have it too.
It can't be all that marvellous . . . '
    Then 'Air with air?' asked Adam, unabashed.
'Total you mix? But show me, how – '
    'I have to go,' the Angel swiftly spoke.
So speaking, he arose. 'Tell me one thing,'
He murmured: 'Can she cook?'


## VIII

'I thought I had no family ties,'
Thus the Ruined Angel sighs.

'But now I find I have a daughter.
By her I find I have a son.
I find my son has children by his mother
(Such sad dogs too).

That makes some family!
Sin and Death and all their progeny.
Not counting Lilith
Whom, truth to tell,
I can't remember well.

Eden's the right place for a family –
Where life is new and easy,
With first-grade fruits from fertile trees.
There shall they be fed
And filled immeasurably.

The present population
Consists of two small upstart squatters,
Childless, as I chance to know.
The greater good of the greater number . . .
Those two will have to go.'


IX

Satan considered the creatures.
Satan selected the serpent.

'The subtle snake, the fittest imp of fraud,'
So spoke the Fallen Angel, fond of artful sound,
So spoke the Fiend, alliteration's friend.

Unfeared and unafraid,
The silken snake lay sleeping . . .

In at his mouth the Enemy entered,
Thorough his throat commodious
Filtered our fatal Foe.

Then up he rose –
As yet the snake stood upright on his tail,
This sleek unfallen fellow,
He surged, not slithered –

And off the Tempter tripped,
And off swept Satan Snakeskin,
In search of silly She.


X

'All this fuss about an apple!
Now, you're a simple woman,'

Said the Snake. 'Like me.
I mean, I'm a simple serpent.

It's a conspiracy of course.
It's meant to keep you down.'

'I don't mind being down,'
Eve tittered.

'Tut-tut,' the Snake tut-tutted.
'Think of higher things!

He only wants to keep you dumb,
And that's the truth.

What's wrong with *knowing*?
Do *you* know what?'

'What's good for talking snakes
Is good for me,' she mumbled,

'Pity to leave it for the birds.'
But the Snake had scarpered.


XI

Eve chomped at the apple
(Her teeth were white and strong:
There was no such thing as decay).
The juice ran down her chin.

She ate it all
(There was no worm at the core:
There was no core).
The juice ran down her breasts.

'I have done something original,'
She told herself.
'But I mustn't be selfish.'
She plucked a second for Adam.


## XII

'What about Adam?
Shall I keep it to myself,
Shall I be on top?

For who, inferior, is free?

But what if I drop dead?
He rushes off and marries someone else.

Good or bad,
Dead or alive,
On top or underneath,
I'd better share it.

I'm a simple woman.'


## XIII

Sighing through all her works,
Nature gave signs of woe.
Earth trembled from her entrails,
Nature gave a second groan.

*

'What's that strange noise?' asked Eve.

'Nothing to worry about,' said Adam.
'Just cataclysms, convulsions, calamities –'

'Don't talk with your mouth full,' said Eve.

'Donner-und-Blitzen, coups-de-foudre, infernos,
Avalanches, defoliation, earthquakes, eruptions,
Tempests, turbulence, typhoons and torrents,'
Said Adam airily.

'And floods. Or do I mean droughts?'
He pondered. 'Also perhaps inclemency.'

'The Snake was right about one thing,'
Eve observed. 'It loosens the tongue.'


XIV

'Must be that Cox's orange pippin,'
Said Adam. 'I do feel queer.'

'I can see that,' said Eve.
'Come over here.'

'Here?'
'Here –

You're good at naming things.
What would you call this?'

Whisper, whisper,
Titter, titter.

'And this –
What would you call this pretty thing?'

Mumble, mumble,
Giggle, giggle.

'Hey, you never did that before!'
'It must be what they mean by sex-apple.'

'Ouch.'
'Mmm.'

'I wish there were ten forbidden trees.'
Snore.

XV

'Where are you, Adam?'

'I'm behind this tree, Lord.'

'What are you doing there?'

'Nothing, Lord. I'm naked is all.'

'Who told you you were naked?'

'I noticed it, Lord.'

'Naked, shmaked, what does it matter?'

'You can get six months for indecency, Lord.'

'What's six months to you, you're immortal.'

'It might give the animals funny thoughts.'

'My animals don't have funny thoughts.'

'The best people wear suits, Lord.'

'You were the best people, Adam.'

'The weather might change, Lord.'

'Too right. It will.'


XVI

'I should have ceased at noon
On the sixth day,'
He said to Himself.
'I think my hand was shaking.

I should have rested content
With the ounce, the libbard, the mole,
With the stag, the river-horse and the bee.

Would the provident emmet
Have eaten the apple?
Never.
Or the gluttonous pig?
Not ever.

The gluttonous pig
Devours his rightful truffle,
He waxes fat,
He is swollen with innocence.

But Eve – that evening's work! –
She alone would eat the apple.
And has she waxèd fat?
Lean and lecherous is she grown.

The ribs of her mate stick out
Like the ribs of a winter's tree,
Its fruits all plucked.
I should have stopped at midday.'


XVII

'The woman . . .'
The Almighty Father shook His head.
'Not like us . . . A new invention.
I blame Adam for what happened.'

'He did it out of love,'
Said the Son. 'An old invention.'

'Love was the first casualty,'
Said the Father, 'Love lies bleeding.'
Adding meaningfully,
'A lot of people are going to be in trouble
Because of love, My Son.'

Then thick as stars
A solemn look on every face
The angels drifted in,
Ending this little tête-à-tête.

## XVIII

*'Son of My bosom,
My Word, My Wisdom, and My Might!'*

'Too easy, loving me.
In me You love Yourself,
Your Word, Your Wisdom, and Your Might.'

*'My sole complacence,
Radiant image of My Glory!'*

'What I mean precisely.
Much further, Father, You must love –
And love what's hard to love.'

*'Too much talk of love.
Die man, or someone else must die.'*

'Account me man *pro tem*.
*Pro tem* account me man.'

Nothing was said about a cross.
By now the quire was in full swing.


## XIX

So the Archangel, out of pity,
Now disclosed the liberal arts
That should relieve man's fallen lot.
'Like music, painting, plays and books.'

'Long books?' asked doleful Adam,
Whom the stern Angel had apprised
Of death and rape and guns and hunger.

'A book there'll be,' the Angel said,
'About this very business –
A poem of ten thousand lines, which one
Called Milton shall compose in time to come.'

'Oh dear!' Then Adam brightened.
'Am I the hero of this book perchance?'
'Not quite the hero,' Michael mildly said,
'And yet you feature largely in it –
God, not unnaturally, is the hero.'
'Should have known,' groaned Adam.

'Although there are – or will be – those
Who claim the hero really is – or will be –
Satan. As I of late foretold,
Henceforth the human race is fallible.'

'That circus snake?' hissed Adam scornfully.
Eve hid her blushes in her work,
A garment she was knitting, made with
Real lamb's wool, tight-fitting.

'In my opinion, which I trust
You won't repeat,' the Angel whispered,
'The hero really is the Son,
Called Jesus, even though his lines
Are fewer in the poem than are mine.'

'And me?' Eve raised her eyes. 'Am I in this –
This book of yours? Or, as I well suppose,
Are all the characters men?'

'Indeed you are!' the genial Angel cried,
'Without an Eve there'd be no tale.
While Mr Milton's not a woman's man,
He does your beauty justice, and your brains.'

'A female intellectual?' Eve grew vexed,
Old-fashioned in her ways as yet.
'No,' spoke the nervous Angel, blushing more,
'I only meant, not just a pretty face.'

Eve held the knitting to her breast.
'By me the Promised Seed shall all restore.'
And Michael knew the time was ripe to leave.
'All – or some,' he murmured at the door.

## XX

There was the escort, in position,
Presenting fiery arms and flaming brands –
Handpicked Cherubim, four faces
To each man and pairs of eyes to match.

'A splendid turn-out!' Eve declared,
Waving graciously.
'Not like our coming in,' said Adam,
Grabbing her wrist.

'Hurry up please!' said the Archangel.
His men were sweating, the Sword of God
Had started the stubble burning.
'We don't want any trouble, do we?'

## XXI

'I had no voice,'
Sighed Adam. 'No real choice.'

Eve wiped a tear and said,
'I wanted you, alive or dead.'

'Whether boon or curse.'
'For better or for worse.'

'Come fair or foul, we have to eat' –
She watched for herbs beneath their feet.

The world lay there, and they could choose.
He said, 'I'll learn to make you shoes.'

## XXII

'Why didn't we think of clothes before?'
Asked Adam,
Removing Eve's.

'Why did we ever think of clothes?'
Asked Eve,
Laundering Adam's.

## XXIII

'What was she like?'

'Who?' asked Adam warily.
'What was who like?'

'Come off it, Adam,
Don't act dumb.
Lilith, of course.
Who else?
Yes, come to that, *who* else?'

'Lilith? Lilith, you say?
Lilith . . . Lilith . . . '

'The one you had before me.
You haven't forgotten already?
The screech-owl –
Was she too much for you?'

'Before you? Fat chance I had
Of having anyone.
Count my ribs if you like.'

'It's common knowledge.
No use your denying it.'

'Oh *Lilith*! – I remember –
The one who shacked up with your fancy man
The Snake.'

'My *what*?
I only met that Snake once in my life.
We only talked.'

'So you say.
As a matter of fact
There's no such woman as Lilith.
The Lord God told me so.'

'First she hangs around with Satan,
Then you tell me she doesn't exist!'

'It's all made up.
It's an old wives' tale.
It's a Jewish conspiracy.'

'So what are you?'


XXIV

'I gave him a very nice name,'
    said petulant Adam.
'I called him SNAKE.
I even gave him a second name,
I called him SERPENT.
There's no gratitude in the world,
They bite the hand that feeds them.'

'The tiger gave me a nasty look,'
    Eve got in quickly.
'The elephant made a vulgar noise,
The cat has scratched my nose,
I found a cockroach in the kitchen.
I'm glad it wasn't me
Who named them!'


XXV

'Death,' said Adam in funereal tones.
'That's the worst of what we've done.
As for the rest of it – that's life.
But Death's a killer.'

'Death?' said Eve, propped on her mop.
'Death would have been deadly in Eden,
Most unsuitable.
But we're not in Eden now.
Other places, other manners.'

'You have a point,' said Adam,
Gladdened. 'It might be held
That, if not exactly vital, Death
Is at all events not wholly inadvisable
In the conditions now prevailing.'

'How well you put it!' Eve admired.
'And may I now remind you
It's time you thinned the carrots out
And there's a lamb to slaughter.'


XXVI

'What's all this
About a sense of sin?
It's rot!' cried young Cain,
'It's the opium of the people.'

'It's all we have, son,'
Said Adam. 'We grew up with it.'
'What's opium?'
Asked Eve suspiciously.

Later Cain killed his brother
For business reasons.
'You see?' his parents said,
'We told you so.'


XXVII

'I told Him flat.
I said: Look here, the ape can't speak to the fish,
The bird can hardly converse with the cat –
How on earth am I to talk to any of them?

I am here, He said, in that way of His. –
Yes, I said, but you'll soon be off.
The country's all right, it's full of nature,
But is it enough?

*Happy*? He said. You mean you want to be *happy*? –
Well, it is my birthright, isn't it?
I could see He was getting ratty.

Very well, He said, fair's fair.
What next I bring shall please thee, I'm no liar. –
An odd expression came over His face –
Thy wish exactly to thy heart's desire . . . '

\*

Then Eve came home from the dentist.
'You're always talking to yourself,
Adam! You should see a psychiatrist.'


XXVIII

Enoch died untimely, he was only 365.
There was bad blood between Adah and Zillah.
Lamech killed a youth in a brawl.
Certain angels got physical.
There was wickedness in tents.
There were giants in the earth.

*

'What about that Promised Seed
You promised?' Adam asked.
'There's a lot needs restoring.'

'Not yet . . . I have a feeling,'
Said Eve. 'Around the year 1000.'

'Hmm,' said Adam. 'Even so . . . '
'It's not something one can rush,'
Said Eve. 'At your age, too!'

'Even so?' Adam asked nicely.
'I have a feeling too.'


XXIX

There were giants in the earth.
Some said they were angels
Lusting after pretty Jewish girls.
Others said they were scholars
(That is, 'mental giants')
Lusting after pretty Jewish girls.

Either way, their offspring turned out ill,
They went to the Devil.
Who had been living in partial retirement,
Teaching himself German:

'Ich bin der Geist der stets verneint! –
Oh very well then, I accept.'

'I knew this would happen,' said God.


## XXX

Jabal had erected the tents,
Jubal was working the hurdy-gurdy,
Tubalcain was running the Ghost Train.

There were crowds of people.
Seth and Enos, Irad and Lamech, Adah and Zillah,
And the sons and daughters of sons and daughters.

There were crowds of people,
There was candy floss and Brighton rock.
It was all go.

'We are making on the swings,'
Said Adam. He was 900 years of age.
Eve counted the takings in silence.
She was slightly younger.

'I'll take a quick look,'
Said Adam.
Coming back, he told her,
'We are losing on the roundabouts.'


## XXXI

'Cities were all right when they were towns,'
Adam grumbled.
'Now it's all rush and noise and pollution.'

'Only this morning I stepped in something
Nasty,' said Eve. 'Left by a dog.
It shouldn't be permitted.'

'Don't blame me then,' said Adam.
'Dogs were always like that.'
Give a dog a bad name, he thought.

'And horses are no better. Look –
Just in front of the house!
You'd wonder where it all comes from.'

Adam rushed for a shovel.
'Can't have you stepping in it, dear.'
It was just the thing for his allotment.

## XXXII

The days of Adam were 930 years.
He sat in the market-place
With other senior citizens.

With Seth, who was just 800,
Enos, who was 695,
And Methuselah, only 243.

'They're not the men
Their great-grandfathers were,'
Said Seth.

'Lamech's kid Noah cries all night,'
Said Enos.
'Howls when they bath it.'

Said the youthful Methuselah:
'They've all been spoilt.
I blame their mothers.'

'It was different in my day,'
Said Adam.
'People lived for ever then.'

## XXXIII

Adam was old bones, lost in his clothes.

Eve thought of how they met. Long,
Long ago. It must have been on holiday.
Warm the air, and full of scents.
And he was wearing nothing, not a stitch.
She blushed a little, pleasurably.

Adam's dreams were not so pleasing.
He woke, delirious and sweating,
Tearing at his twisted nightshirt.

'Eve . . . my side is bleeding . . .
A spear stuck in my side. My rib is hurting.'
'Look,' she said, 'there's nothing there,
No sign at all, dear. Go to sleep.'

He fell back, mumbling indistinctly
About a seed, a promised seed.
She wiped his brow, and smiled:
At heart he'd always been a gardener.


## XXXIV

'The Lord called Adam *Man*.
But Adam called me *Life* itself.

Adam is dead now, man is not.
The Man is dead, but long live man.
For Life goes on.

Priests everywhere, police
And politicians, laying down the law.'
The old girl grinned.

'And I it was who broke it . . .
Poor Adam, poor old Man,
Our sin was self-sufficiency he said.'

Eve did the crossword by her lonely fire.
'That which clasps, a tendril: RIB.'
She died soon after Adam.

# A FAUST BOOK

'Le personnage de Faust et celui de son affreux compère ont droit à toutes les réincarnations . . . J'ai donc osé m'en servir'
– Valéry

'Everyone should write a *Faust* of his own' – attributed to Heine

'Euch ist bekannt, was wir bedürfen,
Wir wollen stark Getränke schlürfen . . . ' – Goethe

# A FAUST BOOK

## *I*

*Dr Faust discourses on the subject of training and heredity*

Out for a healthy walk, Faustus picks
Up a poodle, or vice versa.
A comical little fellow, it chases sticks,
Crawls on its belly, races in circles.

'Perhaps you could train it,' says Wagner.
'No doubt it would respond better
Than many of my students,'
Remarks the Professor.

'Even so,' his assistant ventures,
'There's the question of pedigree.'
'A dog's a dog for all that,'
Says the Professor unctuously.

'To heel, Blackie!' Blackie wags its tail.
'Man's best friend,' says the Professor,
A shade sentimental, it being Easter.
The dog assumes a toothy smile.

## Faust in his study

'The interesting questions go unanswered –
Undue suffering, undeserved success . . .

Divinity talks all the time of better times to come,
Science invents false limbs and true explosives,
And Alchemy turns lead to lead at vast expense;
Art thrills with piggish gods and puffy goddesses,
While Law invokes the laws its lawyers legalize,
And Logic says it all depends on what you mean . . .

So must I live and die in Aristotle's works?'

\*

'Then what is life,'
Faust paced between his piles of parchments,
'Except a slower form of suicide?'

A first-class speaker,
He found himself a first-class listener too.

'This is indeed an honour,'
Yapped the dog. 'I could crouch here
Listening to you for all eternity,
I mean all day.'

'I thought there was more to you
Than met the eye,' said Faust,
Patting him.

'Talking of suicide,' the dog remarked,
'Perhaps I can be of some small service,'
Patting Faust.

*Mephistopheles enlightens Dr Faust*

'Why, if I may ask, did you appear
In the shape of a dog, Mephistopheles?'

'As you will know, our liturgies
Run widdershins, dear Doctor –
A backwards Paternoster,
Commending Cain, rejoicing in Judas,
The Black Mass et cetera.
In my view, often a little vulgar –
Part of the hearts and minds manoeuvre
To win over the masses . . .

So in our parlance the Lord God
Is the Drol Dog,
Ergo, a poodle.
Nothing could be more simple . . .

Talking of which, every god has its day –
What would you like to do with yours?'


*Faust prefers to succeed through his
own efforts, but Mephistopheles
warns him of the obstacles*

'You slog away at it, work, work, work,
Without pulling any strings –
Because your pride won't let you,
Or there aren't any strings to pull.
And at long last you get There –

Looking like the sole runner
In a marathon – first or last?
Your tongue hanging out,
And good for nothing. You made it,
And it unmade you.

And the assembled spectators
Will say, all three of them:
Hurrah, this old fellow got Here
Under his very own steam!

　　　　　(You are leaking from every piston.)
　　　　　They move away, and Here goes with them.

　　　　　We all need someone's help –
　　　　　So why not mine?'

## *Mephistopheles desires a few lines in writing*

'Being of sound mind (and all that mumbo-jumbo), I (name in full) by these presents (already?) do covenant and grant, in consideration of 24 (Twenty-Four) years of service by Mephistopheles, the which (which?) shall bring me anything, or do for me whatsoever, that I give them (names of Lucifer and self) full power to do with me at their pleasure, to rule, to send, fetch, or carry me (that should cover everything) or mine, be it either body, soul, flesh, blood, or goods (curious expression), into their habitation, be it wheresoever (how discreet!) . . .'

　　　　　　　　　　　　　*

　　　　　'Here are the papers,
　　　　　All ready for signature –
　　　　　I'm yours for 24 years,
　　　　　You're mine thereafter . . .

　　　　　Now where's my penknife?
　　　　　Quick, before it dries . . .
　　　　　Blood is thicker than ink,
　　　　　And I hate to strain my eyes.

　　　　　I've immense respect for symbols,
　　　　　They mean a lot to me.
　　　　　Noughts and crosses, for example,
　　　　　And the loaden tree.'

　　　　　(Some other words were heard in Faustus' mind.
　　　　　*There is in love a sweetnesse readie penn'd:*
　　　　　*Copie out onely that, and save expense –*
　　　　　But reason could not tell him what they meant.)

　　　　　'Anaemic forsooth!
　　　　　Lucky I'm not that young Count
　　　　　With a sharp sweet tooth
　　　　　And a taste for throats . . .

Words appearing on your palm?
Sounds most unlikely!
It looks like what they call a Rorschach Blot,
They say it shows your personality.

That's right! –
Now he who runs may read . . .
Oh do stop fussing!
A little spittle clears you of this deed.'


## *The Professor reminisces*

'The likeliest pupil I've had for ages
Was a young fellow called Hamlet,
Foreign but well connected . . .

Not much of a drinker,
But popular with the student body,
And also with the lasses.

An ingenious mind, though always tardy
With his essays . . .
I don't see him as a seminal thinker,

More as a clever *vulgarisateur* . . .
Given the right circumstances,
He ought to go far.'


## *Mephistopheles declares himself a man of the people*

'Myself I favour democracy –
Though as a Prince's man
I can't admit to it openly . . .

It's only right that man should choose freely –
Enjoy pornography of his own accord,
Not be dragged to it like a hijack victim.

Or even make the porn himself
For his own good reasons, like art or money . . .

It's the free agent who interests us,
The rapist – not the raped,
Not normally . . .

Surely the power of election must rest
With the people – of whom there are many.
The process may be time-consuming,
But in the end it eats up . . . more than time.

I was raised among powers and principalities,
But deep in my heart I'm a democrat.
I believe there's a soul in everybody.'


## *Faust rebukes Mephistopheles for his vulgar use of language*

'Knowledge is my bread and butter,'
Faust declared, 'knowledge and truth.'

'Quite,' concurred his affable companion,
Helping himself to more venison.

'The pursuit of knowledge,' said Faust,
Swallowing fast, 'is beset by perils . . .'

'A price on your pate as it were?'
Mephistopheles suggested.

'A manacle on the mind,'
His host corrected coolly.

'I think I follow you –
Adam and his madam paid a price.'

Faust reached for the fruit.
'Precisely,' he said indistinctly.

'They lost a garden,' said his guest,
'But they found a world.'

'At times,' Faust spoke sharply,
'You talk just like a journalist!'

Wagner sniggered. 'Your famulus
Grows familiar!' Mephisto hissed.

## *Faust grows impatient with his companion's dark mutterings*

'You're forever talking rot,' snapped Faust.
'*Which way you fly is hell*, and suchlike . . . '

'And what do you intend,' he groused,
'By *this is hell and you are in it?* –

This is the University Senior Common Room,
And you are in it as my guest!'

'I do repeat myself, I fear,'
His shamefaced friend confessed.


## *Mephistopheles introduces Faust to the fourth estate*

Under the good solid name of Gutenberg Inc.
Mephisto instructs Faust in the art of printing . . .

(The wicked sprites strike up on cue:
    'We have done our best or worst,
    Faust or Fust shall be the first –
    Black letters on white background seen
    Will prove our powder-magazine . . . '
As infantile as ever.)

Whereupon Herr Gutenberg declares himself bankrupt
– 'This fairy gold does tend to depreciate' –
And hands the business over to Dr Faust or Fust.

'I have taught you everything I know,
The rest is up to you, my boy –
Take care of your running head, and
Your tailpiece will take care of itself.'

'There aren't many authors about, ' Faust complains.
'The Imperial Treasury ought to make grants to writers.'

'I know an author,' says helpful Mephistopheles,
'Whose work is out of copyright moreover.'

\*

So Faustus printed the Bible,
In black letters on white background.
And after the copies were all bound
He discovered a word was missing –
'Thou shalt commit adultery.'


'You've turned the Good Book into a naughty one,'
Mephisto laughed. 'I can teach you nothing.'
'You can't get decent proof-readers,'
Moaned Faust, building a bonfire.


He began again, and when the books were distributed
Someone detected a dangerous heresy –
'The fool hath said in his heart there is a God.'
Faust was fined £3000 and the book was suppressed.


'Here's fool's gold to pay a fool's fine,'
Mephisto offered generously.
'You had better specialize in French romances.'


### *Faust requires Mephistopheles to describe hell and heaven for him*

'Tell me, I command you,
What is that place called hell?'

'Hell is grey and has no bottom –
Which reminds me of a joke I heard . . .'

'It was of hell I asked to hear,
Not your stale jokes.'

'But hell is of no substance,
A confused and hence confusing thing –'

'It is yourself that you describe,
I think.'

'So be it – hell is,
Well, it's empty.
Oh there are crowds of people all around.
But hell, you feel, is – empty.
The word is emptiness.'

\*

'Now let us speak of heaven.
What manner of place is that?'

'I lack authority to speak of such.'
(Though not to miss it.)

'Yet you were once in heaven,
Or so I've heard.'

'Some time ago, it may have changed . . .
But – heaven is full.
That's not to say it's chock-a-block with people.
Simply, full – that's what you feel.
The word is fullness.'

'For one renowned for eloquence
I find you sadly tongue-tied!'

'Whereof one cannot bear to speak,
Thereof one says but little.'


## *Faust asks for trouble*

'Now tell me, Mephistopheles – who was it made the world?'
That was a red rag, that would put the cat among the pigeons.
Faustus was flushed with wine, he was feeling foolhardy.

'Ah,' said the other urbanely, 'an interesting question.
There were several of us there at the time, and you know
What these collaborative efforts are. Team-work's the answer.'

## *Faust has doubts about the bargain*

'In return for my immortal soul
I looked for something grander – '
So sighed Faustus, full of dole
' – Than roosters laying addled eggs,
Sour grapes out of season,
And flat beer drawn from table legs.'

Mephisto couldn't say so,
But the going rate for used souls,
Even immortal, was rather low.

'You polished off the grapes for sure,'
He answered drily.
'And don't forget, I helped Old Moore
Predict the grave indisposition
Of a member of the Royal Family –
Likewise Mother Shipton
And the dissolution of the monasteries . . . '

'Poor devil, he's slipped a cog,'
Faust cried jeeringly.
'The monasteries are built on solid rock
And the Kaiser's in his prime!'

'When you've been in hell as long as me,'
His friend wailed piteously,
'You'll find it does things to your sense of time.'


## *Faust journeys to unknown regions*

Dolphins bore Faust to the bottom of the sea.
Dragons swept him into deepest space.

The dolphins carried him back to land.
The dragons brought him down to earth.

'I have been where no man was before!' he cried.
'To be is not to conquer,' sniffed Mephisto.

\*

'And I saw a new heaven and a new earth,'
Faust said. 'For the first heaven and the first earth
   were passed away.'

'I don't think so,' said Mephistopheles, seized
   with unaccountable mirth.
'Not in what we might loosely term your day.'

*

'When you are rested,' Mephisto promised,
'I shall take you to the sage called Freud.
He will guide you on another journey,
He will charm your sins away.'


## *The Doctor displays his erudition in philology*

'Do you mind if we go by broomstick?'
Mephistopheles asked.
'It wouldn't look right, arriving by cab.'

*

'The word *sabbat* or *sabbath*,' said Faust,
'Does not derive from the mystic number *seven*,
As is commonly believed . . .'

'Number seven – go to heaven,'
Mephisto murmured, busy at the controls.

'An amusing though scarcely tenable theory
Has it that the word comes from *Sabazius*,
A Phrygian deity akin to Bacchus . . .'

'Quite a strong head wind,' the pilot grumbled.
'Steeds would have been steadier.'

'But the consensus of opinion has it that *sabbath*
Comes from the Hebrew *shābath*, meaning *to rest* . . .'

'There's no rest for the wicked.'
The pilot corrected a nose dive.
'New brooms don't always sweep clean.'

'My own view, necessarily tentative,
Is that it stems from *saba*, as in *sabaism*
Or *star worship*, properly *host of heaven* . . .'

'In the vernacular,' Mephisto interjected,
'*Army of devils* . . . Bend your knees, please,
We're coming in to land!'

'Interesting word, *knee*: from Germanic *knewam*,
Cognate with Latin *genu*, whence quite possibly
We take *ingenuous*, inclined to kneel – '

*

'I can't see you enjoying the orgy,'
Mephisto scolded, 'with a broken ankle.
For you the word is *shābath* . . .'


*Faust asks another hard question*

'I charge you, Mephistopheles,
Tell me this –
Why is it little children suffer,
Guiltless beyond dispute?'

'It passes understanding,'
             came the pious answer.
'It may surprise you, but in hell
We need to keep child-murderers and molesters
Segregated from the rest. Feelings run high.

No, you can't lay that disgrace on me!
I would rather a millstone were hanged around my neck
And I was drowned in the depth of the sea,
For example.

Even if I'm fishing in the river
And catch a little one, I always throw it back.'

## *Faust is struck by fears for his career*

'There's an academic joke,
A funny story, well, meant to be funny . . .'

'Indeed?' says Mephistopheles glumly,
Not very fond of Faustus' funny stories.

'Well, you see,
A soldier squatting at the foot of the Cross
Says to another:
If the fellow's as bright as you say,
Excellent speaker, always helping people . . .
Then why is he *up there?* –'

Mephistopheles starts laughing.
'Not yet,' says Faust testily,
'I haven't got to the point yet . . .

Then the other soldier says:
Ah, no publications!'

'They came later,' Mephistopheles remarks,
Forgetting to laugh.

'It's a *joke!*' Faust snarls,
'About getting on in the world . . .'

'I thought you were what they call
*Permanent*,' his friend says soothingly.

'But Wittenberg isn't an awfully prestigious
Place . . . I was thinking about Berlin,
The Sorbonne, or even East Anglia . . .

I might produce a book on Metaphysical Evil,
Of course – with some help from you . . .'

'By all means,' his friend replies.
'To coin a phrase – be damned and publish!'

*Mephistopheles reveals the marvels
of science*

This was one of the scientific marvels
Which Mephistopheles disclosed to Faust.

'A sound physicist is a demi-dog,' said he.
'*Ignei, aerii, aquatici, terreni spiritus salvete!*'

Whereupon appeared a vision of muscular demons,
Busy with choppers and chisels in a fiery cellar.

'What are they doing there?' Faust asked.

'They are engaged in splitting the atom.'

'Why should they wish to do such a thing?'

'Why? Because it is theologically impossible,
Because it annoys the Almighty,
And because it makes a devilish big bang –
That's why! . . .

*On kai me on!*'
He dismissed the sweating spirits.
'Myself, I cannot endure loud noises.'


*Faust quizzes Mephistopheles about love*

'But what can fallen angels know of love?'

'We know desire that nothing will relieve.'

'There surely must be whores enough in hell!'

'And all retired . . . My theme is something else.'

'What do you do with love instead of loving?'

'We sublimate our fruitless longing.'

'So hell is paved with high ideals . . . But how?'

'We take an interest in such as you.'

## *Mephistopheles' minions ransack the world's libraries for Faust's gratification*

Mephisto plied Faust with rare books
And curious incunabula.

Such as Aretino's *Sonetti Lussuriosi*,
The *Kama Sutra*, with helpful diagrams,
Homer on Ulysses (a case of mistaken identity),
And some obscure poems about flowers by a Frenchman.

Also *The 120 Days of Sodom*, abridged for busy readers,
A guide to ill-starred taverns called *Lolita*,
*The Story of O* by Oh!
And a checklist of forthcoming titles from the Olympia Press.

(Later, he knew, he would have to do much better,
To less effect.
Leisure would pose a serious problem.)

'Why all this sex stuff?' asked Faust scornfully,
His bed heaped with it.

'You should show more respect.'
Mephisto sounded hurt. 'It was the very first way
Of transmitting original sin . . . '

## *Mephistopheles plays the go-between*

'What is love?'
	Mephisto asked Faust cheerily.
''Tis not hereafter.' (None there embrace.)

'A boy-friend is a girl's best friend,'
	he then told Gretchen earnestly.
'And diamonds next.' (Paste in her case.)

These things were quick to fix.
Faust lived in a big house with lots of space,
Gretchen's cottage was dark and poky.
The sexes lent themselves to sex.
He hadn't really needed jewels. Or poetry.


## *Faust and Gretchen walk in the garden*

'No, I don't see much of the priest –
Actually I'm a Doctor of Divinity myself . . .'

If Divinity was sick
He was the man to cure it.

'Do I believe in God, you ask.
You're a natural philosopher!
Can anyone say he believes in God?
What is meant by *God*?
What is meant by *believe*?
What is meant by *I*?
Can we employ these words any more?'

Gretchen felt that she could,
Though in fact she rarely did.

'But when I speak of *hand*
I know what I mean, I can touch it . . .
Ah, let me kiss it!
What do you mean, I don't know
Where it's been?'

It had been in soap and water.
Her mother took in washing.

'You're not very fond of my skinny friend?
I wouldn't want you to be!'

Gretchen shuddered. Her hand moved
To the crucifix round her neck.

'So you're wearing a cross,
You little darling!
I gave it to you?
Yes of course I did.'

He remembered Mephisto grinning
As he handed it over.
'When in Rome . . . ' the fellow had said.

'It's too good for you?
Nonsense, my sweet – nothing's too good . . .
Oh dear, the chain's broken –
Where can the cross have got to?
It can't have gone too far . . . '

It went too far.


## *Faust is forbidden to marry*

'Remember, there's no marrying
For Bachelors of the Black Arts!'

'But how shall I put it to them?
The subject is bound to come up.'

'You could tell them that you're waiting
For divorce to be invented.'

'According to the book, it is
Better to marry than to burn.'

'The book doesn't say anything
About marrying *and* burning.'


## *Faust is soon bored*

'What drew me so potently
Was her utter innocence.
Now it's gone, gone utterly,
With nothing to replace it.'

He'd eat his crumpet and have it,
Mephisto chuckled. Such a fuss . . .
'But what about experience –
Isn't that a pleasant bonus?'

'That takes time and talent,'
Griped the great lover.
'I don't have the one,
She doesn't have the other.'

*

Mephisto sought to cheer his friend
By telling how in years to come
In a far-off eastern kingdom
Subtle engineers would vend
An artificial maidenhead.

'Made of – I don't know what,
But sold as MATRIMONIAL-BOON,
INNOCENCE-REGAINED, SURPRISE-
YOUR-HUSBAND-WITH-A-SECOND-HONEYMOON . . .
One old fellow will be so surprised
His heart stops on the spot.'

By which date they'd be turning out
Artificial hearts as well, no doubt.

## *A game of consequences*

It had rained the whole day long,
    And Faust was moping.

Mephisto said to Faust:
    'Let's have an evening out.'

Faust said to Mephisto:
    'As long as you're paying.'

So they went to Spicy Spiess's
    In downtown Wittenberg.

There Faust met a go-go dancer
    Called Meretrix, big bust, long legs,

Lusted after by university wits
    And city aldermen alike.

Faust said:
    'I thirst.'

Mephisto told him:
   'Try this Venusberg Lager.'

Meretrix said: 'I'm crazy about theologians!
   Make me an offer I can't refuse.'

Mephisto did, the handsome devil.
   Consequently, there were consequences.


*Mephistopheles remembers the face of God*

'When mankind fell,
They fell into unremembering.

Not so the angels.
When we fell,
We fell into unforgetting,

The flames, the ice,
Its stark unwinking light.

Do you suppose that I
Who used to look upon the naked face of God
Would not do anything
To look again?

Should a ladder stretch to heaven,
Its rungs all razor blades
That slice me to the loins
At every step –
Yet I would do my best
To climb that endless edge,

To look once more,
Then backwards fall
To timelessness in hell.'

'Don't make me cry!' scoffed Faust.
'You hope to curry favour up above?'

'I hope for nothing up above.
Time has rinsed my eyes.
I merely speak the naked truth.'
He knew he could afford to.

Faust already had forgotten.
This talk of naked made him think of Meretrix' bare thighs.


### Faust suffers a temporary indisposition

'The girl's well named,' Mephisto leered.
'First merry tricks, then sorry pricks . . .'

'It's not a joke! I feel unclean.'
He thought of what his mother would say.

Swallows a camel and strains at a gnat,
Reflected Mephistopheles.

No rose without a thorn after all,
It was the price of admission.

'A pity you're not a musician –
They say it's marvellous for creativity . . .'

'You brought it into the world, you devil!
I command you to take it away.'

'Cocksblood!' swore Mephisto. 'Be a man!
I'll soon rid you of your little trouble . . .

> *Shin Aleph Cheth Priapus*
> *summum bonum medicinae sanitas*
>   *spirochaeta pallida*
>   *inferni ardentis monarcha*
> *solamen miseris*
>         *socios habuisse doloris*
> *pox vobiscum*
>         *penicillum –*

There, you're as good as new again!'

*In the tavern*

Oi recken tis a hurenhaus, no good Christchin as all they skivvies ter do is biddin – Baint is biddin they does, tis is beddin – Oi eard tell thikky rum kerl, im that looks loike a yard o pumpen-wasser, do be a flittermaus or vampir – From oly roman vampir eh? ha ha – Meister sends that dirne Gretchen ter fetch the brötchen, bäcker's boy won't go there no more, not after a uge black pudel made a uge black puddle on im – Bäcker's boy be off is loaf anyroads – Ar but there be igh jinx up at doktor's ouse, they say as ow e be makin little babbies in testtuben in is keller – Then what be all they jung mädel fowr? twont niver catch on, could do yerself a nasty schaden wi that there glas – Oive eard orrid noises at noight, speaking in unbekannte zungen loike in church, Oi allus says a vaterunser when Oi goes by – If yer can remember the words, yer betrunken ole bugger – Beim himmel, ere comes is lordschaft isself wi that fancy furriner – Oi be off ome, e played a schmutzig trick last toime, divel take im, turned me wein inter wasser – Haw haw, yer can do that wiout no elp from Ole Nik, yer silly pisswinkel –

*Faust considers the subject of souls*

Gretchen has a large soul and small breasts
Meretrix, great big breasts and a tiny soul
Breasts are of this world: Faust loves them
Faust loves not souls, especially large ones.

*The Doctor's parents journey a great distance
to see their son*

'Dear me, your aged parents have arrived!'
Mephisto winced. 'With lots of luggage too.'

Faustus embraced his mother gingerly.
He took his father's calloused hand with caution.

'I'll get the spare room ready,' Gretchen offered.
Said hearty Merry, 'We can all bunk down together.'

What an outlandish crew! His mother shuddered.
'The ever-womanly must raise or sink you, son.'

'At this time of the year it isn't natural!'
His father poked a peach, his finger went right through.

'We came because we've heard strange stories, son,'
The father said. 'Not nice at all,' the mother added.

'Gossip is a dreadful thing,' Mephisto sighed.
'Smallmindedness and envy,' Faust said airily.

'I don't imagine you'll be staying long?'
Mephisto didn't mean to run a lodging house.

### *Faust's parents question Mephistopheles*

'Where's Miss Gretchen?'
'Gone to church, to pray.'

'Where's Fräulein Merry?'
'Gone to bed, to play.'

'Where's Master Faustus?'
'I wouldn't like to say.'

### *Mephistopheles addresses the working class. Faust's aged parents are nonplussed*

'And your children's children
Shall learn how to spell correctly
How to pen a neat and legible hand
And to read good books

They shall be granted scholarships
And shall suffer therefrom
But they shall succeed in their time
Where their forefathers might not try

And they shall then discover
That correct spelling is held cheap
That the best people hire scriveners
And books are no longer read

Doffing their smocks and overalls
Your children's children
Shall go out to meet the world
And find themselves attired in last year's fashions
(For all things change and remain much the same)
And the world shall ignore them
As hitherto.'

\*

'I can't see what all this
Has to do with our boy Faust,'
Said the aged father.

'I can't see what it has to do
With anything,' mumbled the aged mother.

'It hasn't,' grinned Mephistopheles.
'Your boy Faust has much more going for him –
He has me.'

'I wouldn't mind him being rich,
As long as he was honest,' said the father.

'I wouldn't mind him being poor,
As long as he was happy,' said the mother.

'Youth and age will ne'er agree!'
Sang Mephistopheles, gyrating
On his antique toe.


## *Faust betrays signs of forwardsliding*

'Do you hope to emigrate internally?'
    asked Mephistopheles coldly.
'We have ways of tearing you to pieces.

What's done can't be undone.
What's said can't be unsaid.
Any jackass can repent,
But expiation – that's a literary conceit.
People write it,
They don't live it.

So make the most of what you have,
As we shall.

You cannot take it with you,
As we can.'


## *Mephistopheles calls upon his Master to preserve Faust against the influence of his aged parents*

'Look upon this thy servant Faustus, who is grievously vexed with the wiles of a clean spirit, and grant him pardon of all his residual decencies and inadvertent kindnesses . . . Let thy servant be defended by the sign on his \* of thy Name . . . Drive far hence, O Drol, the pious tempter, and send thy fear upon the tame beast which devoureth the Spillers.

Go out, thou friend of virtue, thou most wicked lamb, the author of marriage, the milkman of human kindness, I adjure thee that thou depart into everlasting temperate conditions . . . '

\*

'I never thought to hear such language!'
  Said the aged father.

'It's what they learn at college,'
  Said the aged mother.

'I'm glad I'm just a humble husbandman,'
  Said the father.

'I'm glad I'm just a humble wifewoman,'
  Said the mother.

'We see that we're not wanted here.'
  The aged father fetched his knapsack.

'Wrap up well, keep regular, dear.'
  The aged mother sniffed a tear back.

## *Mephistopheles salves Faust's conscience*

'A delightful old couple,
But it's for everybody's good . . .
Remember what the poet's bound to say –

> Oh how hideous it is
> To see three generations of one house gathered together!
> It is like an old tree with shoots,
> And with some branches rotted and falling . . .

We wouldn't want our house to be hideous, would we?
We wouldn't want it to rot and fall down?

In ancient Greece – well known of course
As the cradle of western civilization –
Old people were settled in the Underworld.
They could prattle to their hearts' content,
Drink gallons of tea, knit woollies, carve pipe-racks –
And occasionally relatives would visit them . . .

No call to feel guilty, cher Maître!
What was good enough for ancient Greece
Is surely good enough for the Middle Ages.
And that reminds me . . . '

# *II*

## *Faust desires to have as his paramour that beautifull and delightfull peece Helen of Troy*

'Sweet Helen, make me immortal with a kiss!'
Mephisto nods: there was no objection to that.

Golden tresses, swanlike neck and coal-black eyes –
But was she bold and wanton as bespoken?

'Thy lips suck forth my soul: see where it flies!'
Mephisto shakes his head: it should stay where it was.

'That's enough of this youthful idealistic stuff,'
He hisses to Helen: 'You know your business.'

She glares coldly at him, not yet finding her tongue.
She thought her function was to classicize.

## *Mephistopheles and the primrose*

Mephisto smiled at the primrose,
The primrose smiled back.

'A primrose by a river's brim,'
Said Mephisto sanctimoniously,
'A yellow primrose is to him –
Faust, that is –
And it is nothing more.'

The primrose looked unsure.
'But what am I to you, sir?
I feel I can talk to you.'

'To me,' he replied judiciously,
'A primrose by a river's brim
Is something which to him –
I refer to Faust –
Is nothing more than a yellow primrose.'

The primrose dropped a tear,
Or perhaps a drop of dew.
'I just can't win, I fear . . . '

'Cheer up,' said Mephisto.
'I am sure there is someone somewhere
Who regards you as something more
Than a yellow primrose.'

'Oh?' The primrose perked up.
'And who might that be?'

'The Lord God,' said Mephisto.
'After all, he made thee.'

Adding thoughtfully, 'Mind you,
He also made a host of golden daffodils,
To mention but a few.'

## *The Doctor cannot abide gnats*

'Phew!' Faust whistled.
'She's all woman, is Helen!'

'That's nice,' said Mephistopheles.
He was glad there'd been no muddle.

'But she'll have to put away
That Greek tunic.
It's far too revealing.'

'Really?' said his friend,
Who hadn't noticed a thing.

'I can always swallow a camel,'
Faust confided, man to man.
'A camel's a meal –
But a gnat in the throat is hateful.'


## *Faust and the daffodils*

'Top of the morning to you!'
Cried jolly Faustus.

The daffodils tossed their heads,
They too were jocund.

'What a crowd of golden daffodils!'
He exclaimed. 'Or even a host . . . '

The daffodils tossed their heads again.

'One might say you were fluttering
And dancing in the breeze . . . '

The daffodils nodded vigorously.

'But mind your heads don't drop off,'
Said Faustus, bending down.
'Only the best will do for Helen.'

*In extenuation of taking a concubine,*
*Faust pleads vagueness*

'An affair with an immaterial and possibly
Mythical figure hundreds of years old –
How could that get me into serious trouble?
If it were the Rektor's wife I could understand . . . '

'If it were safe there wouldn't be any fun in it,
Would there?' said Mephistopheles.
'Remove the sin from penis and there's not much left,
Is there? You might as well take Origen's tip.'

This is the fellow who calls me trivial,
He thought to himself.
'Do you really fancy the Rektor's wife?' he asked.

\*

'Faust was right,' mused Mephistopheles.
'All this sex isn't getting me far,
And he's even enjoying it . . .

A shady lady with a shady past,
A go-go girl paid well and on the nail,
A silly miss called (save us!) Gretchen . . .

If only I could get him into bed
With one of his students!
But that sticks in his gullet . . . '

But then he brightened.
'Love of course is another matter.
Love calls for concentration –

A thing he hasn't time for.
At least, if I've not harmed him much,
I haven't done him good . . . '

## *Mephistopheles is taken with an excess of zeal*

'Here's a reverend gentleman
Writing a history of witchcraft and demonology –

Demonology! – haven't we gone up in the world!

Now he's describing a "typical witches' sabbath" –
"One cannot write in dainty phrase of Satanists and the Sabbat . . .
This ostrich-like policy is moral cowardice" –

I don't remember any ostriches at our Sabbats . . .

The participants, he says, are subject to
"Mania blasphematoria and coprolalia" –
I wonder what that word means?
All in all it is a "Hellish Randyvous" –
Well said, dear Reverend!

That's what I call first-rate publicity,
Especially the medical bits . . .

I want it in every national and local paper!'

*

(Hundreds of years later it bore fruit
In bodies like the Witches' Liberation Movement,
The Witches' Anti-Defamation League,
And the Witches' International Craft Association.

But Mephistopheles took no joy in this.
Soon there would be no one to liberate,
Or even to defame. Soon there would be no infamy.
He declined to recognize the guilds,
He clung to the virtues of private enterprise.)

## *Faust enjoys further instructive conversations with his friend*

'So you want to do good?
Well, that is good of you . . .

The menu sounds bewitching,
The food tastes like a witch's brew –

Therein lies your difference
Of principle from practice.

To love an idea is easy,
Harder by far to bear with people.

Only as aesthetic phenomenon
Can existence be justified ? –

I don't know what you mean by that,
Unless it's dressing in pretty clothes.

But if your heart is set on doing good,
Don't let me stop you!'

*

'In time to come, you say,
The population will have swollen,
And evil with it.

Kind of you to worry for me.
I know I'm getting on,
An old limb of the devil . . .

True, I see an age ahead
When every card's a self-appointed ace,
And ripe for trumping.

But there is virtue in large numbers,
As well as vice . . .

No call for cataclysms –
A man can lose his soul in many ways,
Not all spectacular.

I have no taste for mass seduction,
Souls carted off on conveyor belts.

I rather see it as an art,
Damnation made by hand to measure.
I fear that I'm old-fashioned.'

## *Mephistopheles' ingenuity displayed*

'Keep us informed of progress!' cried Mephistopheles,
Bursting into the back-room.
'Or even of regress – for we mustn't deceive ourselves.'
He was in the throes of a notion.

They should construct an electronic calculating machine
Capable of analysing the good and evil throughout creation
And providing as it were an up-to-the-minute scoreboard.

The demons were deep in a game of poker.
'Should we include a spiritual breakdown of the animal kingdom?'
Asked one of the players.

'Pray save your sarcasm for an appropriate occasion,'
Said Mephistopheles frostily.

'God sees all,' muttered another. 'Why don't you get together?'
But no one was very worried.
Mephistopheles' crackbrained notions rarely got past Lucifer.

\*

During the Terror, a dedicated young anatomist was preparing heads for dissection by boiling the skin off. A new batch arrived straight from the guillotine. One of them was tonsured. It was the head of a dear friend. (This was engineered by the witty Mephistopheles.) Secretly, while his colleagues were occupied elsewhere, the young anatomist kissed its brow. It seemed to smile at him tenderly. Then he dropped it into the cauldron along with the others. He kept it for himself to dissect, and preserved the skull for several years.

Progress or regress? – the demons wondered. Could that electronic calculating machine have told them? They were often to wonder.


## *Faust is blessed with a son*

Insubstantial though she was,
Helen found herself impregnate
With Faustus' son, named Justus.

'Justus bad as his dad,' Mephisto joked.
He offered to stand dogfather to the babe
But the mother turned her Grecian nose up.

*'Duty, obligation* and *spelling* – '
Announced the proud father, 'the very words
Shall be excluded from his vocabulary!'

Despite the attention lavished on him,
The boy turned out a rebel
With a perverse interest in orthography.

'This infant has no character,'
Faustus complained to Helen.
Mephisto wondered if he had a soul.

*

Later, he took a peasant girl to wife
And succoured his aged grandparents.
They all lived happily a long time after.

He was good with animals, and had green
Fingers, but neglected the Greek authors.
'I prefer true stories,' he would say.


### Helen vanishes

'But she's fading away,'
Faust said in dismay.
'We must send for a doctor.'

Mephisto shuddered.
That was the trouble with shades,
They faded away.

'I can see right through her!'
Lamented Faust.
'Was this the face . . . ?'

Mephisto shrugged.
That was the trouble with cohabitation,
You soon saw through it.

Then one day she wasn't there.
'Gone to Paris for the weekend,'
Mephisto ventured.

But she never returned.

## *Walking in the Harz Mountains, Faust senses the presence of God*

God was a brooding presence.
Brooding at present over new metres.
In which his creatures could approach him,
In which they could evade him,

– And he be relieved of their presence,
Through art as Proxy Divine –
Sublimation, as they termed it,
Which could very nearly be sublime –
For which he was truly thankful.

But how active they were, the bad ones!
They brooded rarely.
They talked incessantly,
In poisoned prose from pointed tongues.
How gregarious they were!
They needed friends to wound.

But who had invented tongues?
(One had to be careful when one brooded.)
And even the better ones
(One had to remember)
Were only human . . .
He started to fashion a special measure
For the likes of Gretchen, a still, sad music.

Creation was never finished.

*Faust has a visitor*

There was a rapping at the door.
'I expect it's for the Professor,' said Wagner.
'Could you take it, Herr Mephistopheles?'
Opening doors made Wagner nervous.

*

'. . . in a nutshell, my respected husband the hochgelehrte Herr Rektor is a renaissance man as they say, his brow is very high and his nose is always in a book, my poor feet are always on the ground of course, when I talk of nature he replies with Nietzsche, I need paraffin, what do I get, I get Paracelsus, he doesn't appreciate my cooking, he reads at table, all this learning, it's bad for the juices, he's a Latin lover, he reads in bed too, Virgil he says, more like vigil I say, it's downright incompatible, he complains of crumbs in the bed, what I complain of is his ologies and osophies, little use they are to a woman in her prime and best nightdress – '

'This way, please,' said Mephistopheles. 'We have an opening for a good plain cook.'

'How dare you, sir! Kindly remember that you are addressing the gnädige Frau Doktor Rektor of Wittenberg, and as for plain, well let me tell you . . . '

*

Eventually she came in.
'But I can't stay long, a woman's work is never done.'


*Mephistopheles encounters the Blessed Boys*

While minding his own business one evening
Mephisto was beset by a chorus of good little spirits.
They hopped and skipped around him, chanting.

    'If the assault be keen
    Fearless must be our mien'
– And so forth.

'Showing their knickers!' Mephisto thought.
'What a terrible thing innocence is . . . '

Soon they were calling him names –
Senile, envious, frustrated, spiteful, impotent . . .
'Reactionary negativism!' squeaked one of them.
'Counter-productive!' piped another.

Obviously from a recent intake.
He gave them a horrid leer:

'You'll look silly when you're my age –
Joints swollen with gout, your haloes moulting,
Lungs gone to pot, and drawers drooping . . .'

He shouldn't demean himself by answering back.
He put out his tongue at them.

'Time for supper!' one of them twittered,
And off they scampered.


## *In the Senior Common Room*

Poor old Schleppfuss, he'd just announced his subject, 'Beauty in a woman is like the gold ring in a sow's nose', when in walked his wife – By the way, has anyone seen Faust recently? – Is he not *corpus naturale* and is not that *mobile*? – Oh, so he's away on sabbatical? – Peripatetic is the word for Faust – Nothing pathetic about him, *wie man sich bettet, so liegt man* – Something's eating him, bills falling due I dare say – Which reminds me, when's the next review of salaries? – The Rektor's in such a foul mood these days one doesn't like to bring it up – Lucky for friend Faust he has tenure – Lucky that nobody's ever defined that clause about *gross insobriety and impropriety* – Ah well, *de minimis non curat lex* – How's your new book progressing? – There's more money in astrology, it's the coming thing – What's the weather forecast? I'm examining at Göttingen next week – Brr, it's been so damned cold we've had to burn our laurel boughs – Yes, time for another bottle of port, I think –

## *Mephistopheles is sorely embarrassed*

'Please,' begged little Justus,
'Tell me what the soul is, Uncle.'

'A fish, my lad, fine and tasty –
You ate one yesterday.'

'You're playing with me, Uncle,
You treat me like a baby.'

'Right-ho, it's what you tread on
As you walk through life.'

'It must mean more than that!
I like true stories best.'

'So, it denotes a state
Of utter loneliness'
(His voice grew bleak)
'Where everything is lost
Save what you never wanted.'

'Forgive me, Uncle,
I cannot think that you are wholly right.'

'I'm not far wrong,' Mephisto snapped.
'Why can't you be like other boys
And play at tearing wings off flies?'

'Uncle dear, do flies need wings
Because they have no souls?'

Mephisto sweated. This was how it felt
To be a family man. 'Look, laddie,
This uncle is a Harmful Influence –
You'd better cultivate your Uncle Wagner.'

He turned and hurried off.

## *Mephistopheles relates a tale of olden times*

'So that very night,' said Mephistopheles in a
   confidential whisper,
'I slipped into the bedchamber of Pilate's wife –
A remarkably handsome woman, I may say – '

'Yes?' said Faust, hanging on every word.
'And what did you do? Did you do it?'

'Oh, yes, I certainly did.
I snuggled up close to her, on the pillow –
What an opulent figure she had! – her name was Claudia,
   by the way – '

'Do get on with it!' Faustus was twitching.

'And I whispered a dream in her ear –
Exquisitely shaped it was, her ear I mean, like a shell,
   only much softer of course – '

'Never mind her ear – a dream did you say?'

'A trick of the trade. We tried it on Eve –
She had a fine ear too, sort of pink and innocent –
But we were caught then, we were only beginners.'

'Never mind Eve – what about this dream?
Didn't she wake up?'

'I put it to her – Claudia, that is – in fictional form
And with lots of strong emotions like you get in dreams,
That she should prevail upon her lord and master –
He was snoring in the next room, I was glad I wasn't whispering
   in *his* ear – '

'I do wish you'd hurry up with this story!'

'– and get him to stay the execution of Jesus and
Remit the sentence to thirty years of digging wells
   in the desert . . . '

'That was high-minded of you,' said Faust, abashed.
'I trust you got something out of it?'

'The idea was to avert indiscriminate redemption,
Of course.' His voice fell. 'But it didn't come off.
It seems Pilate's wife was always having dreams –
Fancy that! he'd say at breakfast, but he never listened.'

## *Faust is troubled by a dream*

Faustus dreamt a strange dream, strange and deathly.
In his dream he heard the voice of a small lady,
Piping perhaps, or perhaps chanting chillingly.

'Aroint thee, false witch!' cried she with a brave face.
'Human inventions help properly, magic is a disgrace.'

Still shaking, Faustus told his dream to Mephistopheles.
'It was a poem,' said the latter, 'and only meant to tease.'

In actual fact, he continued, the lady in question
Was the proud owner of a mighty and intricate engine,
A Washing Machine, which cleansed and rinsed one's linen.

'By no means pure magic, but merely applied.
Nothing at all to be scared of, my son –
Before long no home will be complete without one.'

'Human inventions are nicer,' Faustus opined.
'For Gretchen's a dab at wash-tub and flat-iron,
The Frau Rektor can cook a tiptop hotchpotch,
And even Meretrix is good at shelling peas . . .'

'But you are privileged,' said Mephistopheles
Indulgently. 'You have the magic touch.'

## *Faust appears before the Senate*

Addressing the Senate of Erfurt,
Faust offers to restore various lost masterpieces
For as long as it takes to make copies.

Among them,
The missing comedies of Terence and Plautus,
The complete works of Sappho –

'I have four teen-age daughters,'
One of the senators starts to protest –

Aristotle's *Customs of the Barbarians*,
Homer's *No Second Troy*, or Post-war Developments,
And Cinna's verses for which he was slain.

'Very interesting,' says the chairman, 'I'm sure.
But our clerks are under considerable strain
What with minutes, motions and amendments . . .
However, we shall make a note of your kind offer.'

'Hear, hear,' mumble the senators.


## *Wagner is anxious*

'What is amiss with my master?
Once the lecture theatres rang with his *sic probo!*

He rarely takes his classes these days.
He's always on the wing –
Off to an international conference
Or advising foreign governments –
Or closeted with that – that Levantine,
   I suppose . . .

Or else relaxing with a lady.
Well, that's all right, it's normal,
   I suppose . . .

But how I used to relish his *sic probo!*
I like things being proved.
I like plain honest truths.
One day perchance I'll marry a plain wife,
A nice shy ordinary girl.
Trouble is, I'm shy too – how shall we get started?

*Sic probo!* I shall say to her, and kiss her.
But firstly I must get my teacher's licence . . .
I wish my master hadn't grown so young.'

## Gretchen at the sewing-machine

'My stomach is sore,
My peace is fled,
I wish I'd been careful,
I wish I was wed.

Once I would scold
A poor girl in disgrace,
Now it's for me
To hide my face.

I love him still,
My dear Johannes,
His clever words,
His polished manners.

It's not surprising,
When I love as I do,
That those more knowing
In love, love him too.

There's no one to help,
I can't tell my mother,
The priest would be shocked,
I'm scared of my brother.

He says his religion
Forbids him to marry,
If only I
Had the luck to miscarry!

Perhaps his crony,
That creepy fellow,
Could tell me of someone
Or somewhere to go.

My stomach is swelling,
My peace is fled,
I wish I'd been careful,
I wish I was dead.'

*Faust exhibits his necromantic powers*

At the Duke of Parma's court
Faust performed unheard-of feats of magic.

He summoned spirits to enact
Goliath slain by David,
Judith beheading Holofernes,
Samson bringing down the house,
The Vandals sacking Rome . . .

The courtiers were enthralled.
'Unheard of!' they exclaimed. 'Unseen as well!'

But Parma's Duke spoke sternly:
'This circus is for common folk!
Have you no power to raise our minds
With shows of nobler deeds,
But only rapine, death and ruin?'

Faust bowed his head in shame,
And packed his raree-show.

At the gate the major-domo waited.
'His Grace desires to see in private
Adam with his bride before the Fall,
Mars and Venus caught in Vulcan's net,
King David and his virgin side by side,
And Cleopatra's nights of love . . .
He'll make it worth your while.'

'Humble regrets,' said Faust, 'the show is over.'


*Lucifer broods*

'It was quite simple –
If God could be god
Why couldn't I?

All I asked for
Was equality and independence,
*Primus inter pares* –

With not too many *pares*.
A rotating chairmanship
Might have been the answer.

What happened to the question?

Better to reign in hell than serve in heav'n –
But better still to reign in both.

What, you might ask, is the point of it all?
Seduction, corruption, ruination –
All this hard labour I put in,
Day after night after day

– The solace of having companions . . .

Companions! Do these lost souls
Imagine they're as good as me?
Damn their eyes!

So I am the Spirit who always says No?
Once I was ready to say Oh yes!'

\*

'I do wish he would stop brooding in my head . . .
Where are the aspirins?' Mephisto whispered.
'God knows!' yelled Meretrix.


### *The political achievements of Faust*

A waste of time it would be, dear reader,
To itemize Faust's political feats,
For in effect they were no whit brighter
Than his infamously vulgar leg-pulls –
Like turning a horse to a bale of hay
Or invisibly tweaking the Pope's nose . . .
Granted, he assisted the Count of X
To repel the powerful Duke of Y
With empty suits of armour and false fire –
But neither Count nor Duke was gratified:
Honest war it wasn't, for no one died.

He furnished the Z Republic with a
Computer called Rational Government.
Its rule was just, taxes were abolished,
Crime dwindled, the economy flourished –
And the good citizens were bored to tears.
Vast Indian stretches he saved from floods,
Only to see them laid waste by a drought.
When he clad all the students in silk and
Velvet, they quickly returned to their rags . . .
Thus Faust did good, as he had wanted, and
Little good came of it. Angry he grew
And embittered, but Mephistopheles,
His faithful helper throughout, merely smiled.


## *Mephistopheles lectures in the Professor's stead*

'Your attention please, Studenten and Studentinnen –
We now come to the final scene of this curiously set text.
I shall ask you to evaluate in passing the random contingency of
   metonymic association and the substitutive totalization by
   metaphoric reversal . . .
No, I shall not repeat that, if you can't grasp it first time
   you shouldn't be here.'

To his horror he spotted the gang of blessed boys
   fidgeting in the back row.

'Mountain Gorges, Forest, Cliffs, Wilderness –
All the machinery of advanced Sturm und Drang, you will
   observe, in a semiological mishmash of arcadian and religiose.
Holy anchorites are paradoxically said to be on the move,
   while a Pater Ecstaticus hovers in the murky air . . .
And what, pray, is a Pater Ecstaticus?'

'A happy father,' said one of the cursed boys,
   'who has just had his eldest son and heir.'

Mephistopheles continued briskly:
'Various grades of angels make their appearance, some young,
   some old, some less perfect, some more so, but all talking big
   as per usual . . .'

'Hey look!' shouted one of the dreadful youths,
   'We come next – let's see what you make of us!'

'The *seligen Knaben* or Boys' Brigade seem to be doing
   something obscure but nasty to a dumb chrysalis – a deplorable
   concession to public taste.'

'Old phoney! Doesn't know what he's talking about!'
Somebody let off a fire-cracker.

'Explain please to us the Magna Peccatrix,'
   asked a pale-faced student from Fribourg.
'Is it possible she is a referent purely symbolic?'

'Il ne s'agit pas d'une nouvelle affaire Marguerite –
That's certain. Look it up for yourself: Luke, vii.
The plain fact is – '
He paused to consider what the plain fact was.

' – that, despite a flimsy story line, the author has introduced a
   surfeit of characters and failed to distinguish between them – '

He took a deep breath.
'Mulier Samaritana, Maria Aegyptiaca, Una Poenitentium
   (what a mouthful!), the epicene Doctor Marianus, and a
   Mater Gloriosa, presumptive wife to Pater Ecstaticus.'

He sighed.
'You will have noted a deficiency of realism in the work,
   and a lack of relevance to the here and now.
And the scene now comes to an end, not before time, with
   an apt allusion to women and the ineffable . . .
This lecture also comes to an end, because I have a symbolic
   headache.'

The blessed boys were making disgruntled noises.
'Resign!' they were heard to advise, 'Resign!'

## *In sorrow Wagner takes his leave of the Doctor*

Wagner was offered work at Heidelberg,
Coaching some student princeling.

Loath though he was to leave his master,
He had to think about his future.

'Che sarà,' he told himself, 'sarà.'
But tears were standing in his eyes.

'I no longer feel at home here, Doctor.
I was ever ill at ease with ladies,

And your strange friend gives me the shivers.
Last night as we played snakes and ladders

The board began to writhe and hiss –
"My favourite game," he cackled, "snakes and adders."

Forgive me, sir, but I must go from here,
And if I may, I wish that you would too.'

'So be it,' Faustus sighed and shook his hand.
'Then may you teach as well as you have learned.'

## *The prophecies of Mephistopheles*

Of the worm Tyranny, which shall be chopped down
 and into a thousand pieces

Concerning the miserabilism of the Jews
 who may never turn away a pregnant female

That as Leben by Nebel, so shall Live be contained
 by its contrary,
And there shall be no life without file

Of the abolition of inferiority
 in so far as is consistent with superiority

Of the discovery of humanism,
 leading to a love of cats, dogs and aquarium fishes

That many shall drown in the depths of their skin

Concerning nations which speak with one voice
    and likewise scrawl on walls

That when there is no longer room for lying down
    mankind shall couple standing up

How alchemy shall yield to chemists, aspiration to
    aspirin, barbs to barbiturates, aesthetics to
    anaesthetics, whores to hormones, heroines to heroin

That even as men have created women,
    so shall women destroy men

That a God all-merciful is a God unjust,
    and that God will be just

How Faustus shall live for ever
    and Mephistopheles a little longer

That only those prophecies are genuine
    which show a profit.

## *Faust is interrogated by the authorities*

A noise like thunder was heard at the door.
'Open at once in the name of the law!'

'It's open already,' replied the Professor.
'You need only apply the gentlest of pressure.'

'I am the Polizei Kapitän Scheister,
And with me is our esteemed Bürgermeister.'

'So pleased to meet you! Let's all have a drink.'
Mephisto snapped his fingers. 'Schnapps, I think.'

'We've had lots of complaints,' said the grave Polizei. –
'It's the weather,' sighed Mephisto, 'first wet and then dry.'

'I must ask this Herr to show us his Ausweis!
We're on the qui vive for spies in disguise.'

A cunning devil is never caught short.
'Take your pick – I've a pass for every port.'

'The neighbours complain about accents unholy!' –
'We're translating the Good Book into Swahili.'

'The game's up, Doktor, you might as well tell us
What you are up to down in your cellars!'

'Atomic mushrooms,' his proud friend replied,
'Coming on nicely – I adore them when fried.'

'And where is the mädchen by the name of Gretchen?' –
'Buried of course in the basement, mein Kapitän.'

'You think we policemen are boobies, ha ha!
She's really gone out for a walk, nicht wahr?'

'Brilliant!' cried Faustus. 'You're hard to deceive!
Now please mend the door before taking your leave.'


## *Faust desires to meet Lucifer*

'I would dearly meet your Master.
Perhaps he'll throw more light than you can
On life's dark matters.'

'Lucifer brings light, but darkness too.
If you suppose that I am – as you say – designing,
You ought to meet my Master!
Lord of ambiguity, Shade of many a meaning,
Spectre of the spectrum, the Giver and the Taker . . .'

He found it hard himself to comprehend his Master.

'I'm the practical party. Straight and homely,
    though not insignificant.
But I expect you'll meet him one day, dearly.'

## *Faust is set upon by Gretchen's brother*

One dark night Faust and Mephistopheles come face to face with Gretchen's brother in a deserted alley. He is a soldier, on compassionate leave, and called (such is the fancifulness of the lower orders) Valentine. 'Here's trouble!' mutters Mephistopheles. 'He's heard about his sister.' Valentine pulls out his sword. 'You swine!' he cries, among other rancorous and trooperlike ejaculations. Mephistopheles tells Faust, 'I'll keep him busy, then you stab him, preferably in the back, with – what do you have on you? – a quill, a piece of chalk, a forefinger – anything will do the trick.'

Mephistopheles and Valentine begin to fence. Clash, clash! Mephistopheles makes a sign, and Valentine's sword-arm is instantly paralysed. 'Magic does have its uses,' Mephistopheles pants. Faust steps bravely forward and runs Valentine through with an outstretched finger. Valentine falls, crying out, 'My sister – a strumpet!' And dies. 'Officer,' says Mephistopheles in a posh voice as the Watch comes round the corner, 'there's a poor fellow lying here and wishing for a trumpet – to play the Last Post, I fear.'

\*

'It was two against one,'
Moans the Doctor,
'Unfair competition.'

'All's fair in love and war,'
Says the other,
'And this was both. What's more,
He was a professional
While you're an amateur.

Better a living amateur
Than a dead professional.'


## *Faust finds it is later than he thought*

'Not twenty-four,' said Mephistopheles,
'But twelve years only if you please.'

'The pact,' Faust shouted, 'calls for twenty-four,
As I can prove in any court of law!'

'Your calculations must have gone astray –
You used my services by night as well as day.'

'You're nothing but the cheapest sort of cheat!'
Faust cried.

'A cheat I well may be, but I'm not cheap,'
His friend replied.

'By night I slept,' Faust said, 'and so
Did you, you dog, for all I know!'

'Indeed you slept – you slept with Gretchen,
With Helen, with the go-go girl from town –

You always rose to the occasion,
Because I never let you down . . .

And if you only dreamt at night,
Who made your dreams but I? –

Oh, I worked double time all right!'


*Faust asks himself what he has gained*

'The fool, they say, persists in his folly.
So does the proud man in his way –
It may be folly, but it is his own.
While still man strives, still must he stray.

And if the proud man throws good money
After bad, at least this will proclaim
His disrespect for riches,
Or prove the justness of his aim.

To save his intellectual honour
The clever man cuts off his nose –
Who knows, his noseless face may grow in stature,
Or else some grander nose may grow?
While still man strays, still shall he stride.

I told this hound of hell,
This pitman paid to help me strive,
That I would learn
    why it is the guiltless suffer,
    and why the wicked thrive –

His answer was: "As you discern,
God moves in a mysterious manner –
Unlike me. Me you can understand."

But now I think that I have understood
Whether or not the guiltless always suffer,
Not all the wicked always prosper.

And I shall write this in my blood.'


## *Faust makes his will*

'After the specific legacies herein entered
    have been disposed of,
I devise and bequeath the residue of my estate
To Madam Meretrix for her absolute use and benefit'
(Meretrix saw to that)

'My second-best bed I bequeath to Fräulein Gretchen,
    of address unknown'
(She lived far off, with a man who wanted children)

'To the Frau Rektor of Wittenberg University
    I leave the Herr Rektor of Wittenberg University'

'To Master Wagner, my faithful clerk,
Whose counsel I have cause to regret ignoring,
    I leave my books,
Among which are some he is entreated to burn,
Also my ink-horn and my gold hunter for which
    I have no further use'
(*Terminat hora diem*, Wagner would say, tapping it)

'My son Justus Faustus I cut off without a penny,
    for the good of his soul'

'To my incorruptible parents
  I leave their pleasanter memories of me'

'To Johann Gutenberg, if he can be found,'
(He could never be traced)
'I demise the sum of twenty-four guilders,
  for it must seem his guilt'

'A certain immaterial item has been assigned
By separate instrument to Herr Mephistopheles:'
(Much good might it do him)
'Being without prejudice to Madam Meretrix' interests,
  this need not be specified here . . .'


*Mephistopheles assures his companion
of immortality*

'Why did I not give up the ghost
When I came from my mother's belly?'
Thus lamented Faust.

                *

'But you're lucky, Doctor,
You are privileged,
You'll be remembered –

Not exactly in flowing cups,
But in story-books,
A play or two, an opera perhaps . . .'

(He saw the stage machinery running
Amok, dragons and heaven collapsing,
Killing two or three of the actors –
Yes, that was at Lincoln's Inn.

And in a town called Exeter,
One devil too many on stage
Who didn't seem to be a player –
He would enjoy that.)

'In fact a noble Engländer
The Duke of Ellington
Will put you in an operetta
With a cute mulatto Helen!

Pity about your name though,
Doesn't have much of a ring to it.
Mephistopheles now –
There's music for you . . .

But you're fortunate, Faust,
You should count your blessings –
Most lost souls don't rate an epitaph.'

## *Faust's farewell to his friends*

'We'd all had formal invitations. Must be something weighty, the Dekan remarked as we went in. He started badly, I'd never heard him stutter like that. My trusty and well-beloved friends, he said at last, Hear me with patience and take warning from my story. Naturally people began to titter. He mumbled something concerning wicked exercises and conjurations, and how his mother was right . . . and his contract, and murder and lechery, and being wedded to Lucifer. The Rektor walked out at that point. Maybe it's poetry, my neighbour whispered. But it didn't rhyme. There was an hourglass in front of him. The sands are running out, he cried. By now most of the audience had too. I heard him say distinctly, Hell has many mansions, each with a single bed. Then he howled, He will fetch me! and fell against the lectern, crashing to the ground with it. I hurried to him, but that weird friend of his was there first. He growled something about drink on an empty stomach, hoisted Faust over his shoulder and rushed off with him. Yes, it was a sorry business.'

*Lucifer advises Mephistopheles of the device known as sprats and mackerels*

'Someone in Weimar has tacked together
An artful defence of your friend, I gather.'

It was Lucifer speaking.
He was speaking out of a cloud.

'It seems that Faustus was only striving –
And to his Lordship striving is pleasing.'

'I strove – and he succeeded!
That tale won't cut much ice in hell!'

'I think we yield to the cunning Geheimrat,
And suffer your fortunate friend to depart.'

'You want us to look foolish, Lucifer?
How can you do this to your servant? –
It's devilish!'

The cloud that Lucifer spoke out of
Grew darker. So did his voice.

'We all have our cross to carry,
But crosses are ladders.
We let the Doctor go scot-free,
To encourage the others . . .

*Experto credite!*'
The storm-cloud drifted away.


*Mephistopheles wonders*

His Master had too much on his plate,
Mephisto reckoned. It was beyond a joke –
Couldn't see the trees for the forest fire,
Sometimes spoke in a cloud of smoke.

Yet did Mephisto want Faust?
Maybe Rachel was worth those years
   of Jacob's labouring –
But the soul that could be purchased
Was rarely worth the having.

'If it had been Justus, now . . .
Or the aged parents, he or she,'
He shuddered slightly.
'Or even Gretchen, even Wagner . . .'

It was always the one that got away
You ended by wanting.
Sometimes he thought his work
Wasn't very satisfying.

Sometimes he wondered
Who he was working for.


### *The commander dismisses his troops*

The times were out of joint,
Ancient custom gone by the board . . .
The troops were standing to.

'Stand down, platoon!
Fat fiends with blunt horns
And lean ones with broken ones . . .
No, stand up, you lumps!

The mission has been aborted.
It's roses roses all the way for Faust . . .
So hand in your pitch and brimstone –
And wipe those looks off your faces!

No muttering in the ranks!
Yours not to reason why.
If action's what you want,
Then go chase the blessed boys –

Or girls for all I know, the Gestümper!
And find out what they're made of.

But remember, just rough them up,
We don't want a diplomatic incident.'

Poor devils, he thought.
It was a question of morale.

## *Faust and Mephistopheles make their adieus*

'We too can move in a mysterious way,'
He ground his teeth. 'Once in a while –
So don't pin your faith on it!

I shall tear this contract into pieces.'
He did so, very slowly.
'You're free. If free's the word . . .

I scarce expect a testimonial,
But can't you make a special effort
And just for once say Thank you?'

Faust thought of how his hand had hurt.
'Thank you,' he said at last.
'I'm not entirely taken by surprise.'

'Indeed?' The other strove to look
Entirely unsurprised. 'Mind you,
You only gain what we are glad to lose –

Time, and time hangs heavy.
You'll miss me, Faust. I was your muse.
Who will amuse you now?'

The one considered things to do in time.
The other thought of things that time could do.
The stars stood still, the clock marked time.

'That's true, my friend,' Faust sighed.
'You've ruined me for other company.
I'll pass my days in some far wilderness.'

Was there no wilderness at hand?
'I'll miss you too,' said Mephistopheles.
'But then, I'm used to missing . . .'

# OXFORD POETS

Fleur Adcock
Moniza Alvi
Joseph Brodsky
Basil Bunting
Tessa Rose Chester
Daniela Crăsnaru
Michael Donaghy
Keith Douglas
D. J. Enright
Roy Fisher
Ida Affleck Graves
Ivor Gurney
David Harsent
Gwen Harwood
Anthony Hecht
Zbigniew Herbert
Tobias Hill
Thomas Kinsella
Brad Leithauser
Derek Mahon
Jamie McKendrick
Sean O'Brien

Alice Oswald
Peter Porter
Craig Raine
Zsuzsa Rakovszky
Henry Reed
Christopher Reid
Stephen Romer
Eva Salzman
Carole Satyamurti
Peter Scupham
Jo Shapcott
Penelope Shuttle
Goran Simić
Anne Stevenson
George Szirtes
Grete Tartler
Edward Thomas
Charles Tomlinson
Marina Tsvetaeva
Chris Wallace-Crabbe
Hugo Williams